Elian McCready's
NEEDLEPOINT

Elian McCready's
NEEDLEPOINT

David & Charles

For Noel, Ivan, Titus and Anna,
and in memory of my mother

A DAVID & CHARLES BOOK

First published in the UK in 2002

Designs Copyright © Elian McCready 2002
Text, photography and layout Copyright © David & Charles 2002

A catalogue record for this book is available from the British Library.

ISBN 0 7153 1150 6

Executive commissioning editor Cheryl Brown
Executive art editor Ali Myer
Desk editor Sandra Pruski
Book design Lisa Forrester
Project editor Linda Clements
Charting Ethan Danielson
Photography by Lucy Mason, except
page 7: Nic Barlow and page 32-33: Debbie Patterson

Printed in Singapore by KHL
for David & Charles
Brunel House   Newton Abbot   Devon

CONTENTS

Introduction 6

PEONIES AND HOLLYHOCKS WALL HANGING 8

COCKADOODLEDOO CUSHION 16

FLOWER MINIATURES 24
IRIS MINI CUSHION 26
PANSY MINI CUSHION 28
TULIP MINI CUSHION 30

NAXOS CAT CUSHION 32

CARMEN MIRANDA CUSHION 38

FLEMISH FLORALS 44
MORNING GLORY CUSHION 46
ROSE TEACOSY 51

MANDARIN DUCK CUSHION 54

NASTURTIUM WAISTCOAT 60

FROSTED GRAPES STOOL 70

ALFRESCO TRIO 78
ALFRESCO GRAPES CUSHION 80
ALFRESCO LEAVES CUSHION 81
ALFRESCO WALL HANGING 90

IRIS PANEL 96

PANSY SLIPPERS 106

ORCHARD BOUNTY 112
APPLES BAG 114
APPLES AND PEARS CUSHION 115

Materials, Techniques and Making Up 122
Acknowledgments 127
Suppliers 127
Index 128

INTRODUCTION

My earliest artistic influence was my mother, an amateur painter and intuitive colourist with a passion for flowers. My own creative pursuits continued while I raised a family, worked in the wardrobe department of the BBC, and finally completed a degree in Fine Art. Years living in the country introduced me to spinning and weaving and the discovery of pictorial woven tapestry – a synthesis of Fine and Applied art. It opened up a whole new world.

Sometime in the 1960s I chanced upon a book called *Woven by Hand* about a group of weavers at the Ramses Wissa Wassef School in Egypt. Their unique and beautiful work uses a technique called 'eccentric weave' that results in an undulating free-flowing style. So when, in 1985, I received a Winston Churchill Travel Fellowship, I seized the opportunity to visit the Wissa Wassef school. Students are encouraged to work straight on to the loom, resulting in huge works of great complexity and glowing beauty. They've haunted me and ever after I've been in search of that same lively, intuitive impulse in my own work.

Another major artistic influence was Kaffe Fassett, of whom I had always been a huge fan, admiring his creative energy and bold style. When my urge for development took me to London he offered me work, and at his studio, where stunning floral chairs and rugs in needlepoint were being designed, I found my *métier*. The pictorial element suited my painterly aspirations, and needlepoint became all-consuming. The years I spent there were a real learning experience, challenging and rewarding: a landmark in my career.

Since 1991 I've designed in my own name, mainly for Ehrman. I generally paint my designs first, full scale in acrylic, and so have the joy and satisfaction of indulging in both media. I can feel ill with disappointment if a design fails to work out, or near drunk with elation when it succeeds. The methodical progress of tent stitch can be frustrating as creative ideas run ahead. Long stitch gives me the chance to spread my wings and work with broader strokes of colour, as can be seen in the Iris Panel on page 96.

Sometimes an idea will lie in wait for years, like the small sketch I used for an earlier wall hanging and which was much later an inspiration for the Nasturtium waistcoat in this book. I keep bulging files of cuttings, hundreds of postcards, books, china, fabrics, shells. I stuff anything into vases and bowls, from round onion seed heads to pampas grass or plastic flowers. I buy marrows and pumpkins and plums and pile them on big yellow plates – some to eat and some 'for the house' – like the huge orange pumpkin which sits atop our kitchen table on a green-spotted blue cloth and is replaced each year, a constant still life. Treasured plates all go up on the wall. I never take a walk without bringing home more booty to pile on yet another surface. This magpie-like urge to hoard and display is difficult to live with, but does create a storehouse of constantly shifting arrangements of form and colour that inspire me.

The preparatory art work is problem-solving time, when all my attention is given to the drawing, the composition, and the general balance of darks and lights. I love this bit, and don't generally think about the needlework too much. Inevitably there's a degree of compromise later, but the challenge of translation is an interesting one. Occasionally I struggle to find the right wool (yarn) and discover instead a juxtaposition of two colours that will interact visually on the canvas: perhaps an acid yellow and a pale green that give an illusion of lime. If the pinks are too cool, I try a few yellow or orange stitches. I seldom use true black: there's much more warmth of tone in dark plum or maroons.

My designs explore the natural world. The first needlepoints to earn me recognition were outsize flamboyant flower pieces in long stitch – the Peonies and Hollyhocks wall hanging is just such a design. Even the humble pansy can aspire to grandeur when seen on a big scale. I've done the same with nasturtiums, tulips and roses which intrigue me by their form, their gestures, their grace. Fruit is a simpler architecture but no less challenging. I relish modelling its rounded forms and suggesting texture and gloss with murky shadows and soft highlights, as can be seen in the Alfresco trio of designs on pages 78–95 and the Carmen Miranda cushion on page 38.

I like things to overflow their boundaries – take the eye beyond the frame. Certainly in the crowded flower and fruit designs I cram in so much that only small negative shapes of background remain. I employ exaggeration to create drama; colour I use emotively to the same effect; and the drawing is the backbone of the work, giving structure and authority.

Needlepoint is a solitary business – weeks, if not years of my life are spent in working alone. Progress is slow. There are disappointments, panics and frustrations, but there is also the rich reward of producing something uniquely my own. This is a book about inspiration – my personal journey into art and textiles and my quest for a personal voice.

Elian McCready

PEONIES AND HOLLYHOCKS WALL HANGING

Late in the 13th century, the Italian traveller Marco Polo visited the court of Kublai Khan in Xanadu, China and was overcome by the splendour of the gardens, though Europeans refused to believe his reports. Peonies were first cultivated thousands of years ago in the imperial gardens of China and given such regal and splendid names as 'King of Flowers' and 'Hundred Ounces of Gold'. The Chinese regard the peony as the herald of spring, a symbol of the month of March and an emblem of love and affection, encapsulating the yang and ying principles of male and female beauty.

The extraordinary beauty of the peony made it a favourite motif in the decorative art of the Far East, frequently depicted with butterflies or the Chinese lion. Huge, ruffled blooms adorn porcelain, fans, screens and stunning silk scrolls. Kimono decoration, one of the most beautiful of Japanese art forms, regularly featured the ornamental peony.

The hollyhock also originated in China, its tall, stately spires now the glory of English country gardens. A member of the mallow family, it has been used in folk medicine and takes its name from the Greek 'to cure'. In Japanese art, the hollyhock adorns pottery and appears with stylistic simplicity across decorative screens. In Dutch flower painting it was a recurring motif in exuberant bouquets, sometimes having a shadowy profile at the top of these layered flower pieces, and sometimes a dominant role alongside other tall flowers like the iris and the crown imperial lily.

The narcissus was another standard ornamental motif in both Japanese and Dutch flower painting. It comes from

the Mediterranean and takes its name from the Greek *narkao* (to benumb) on account of its narcotic properties and not, as is commonly held, from the vain youth who fell in love with his own reflection.

Peonies and Hollyhocks Wall Hanging

IN THIS LONG STITCH HANGING, I've borrowed from the Dutch and Oriental tradition by juxtaposing flowers that would not bloom together in nature. Hot pink peonies dominate while smouldering maroon hollyhocks form a strong vertical at the right-hand edge, their saucer shape described by the blue light catching their petals. The fresh, creamy narcissi provide a rhythmical link and a touch of delicacy and light. This design was initially painted full size, in careful detail, and long and short stitch has been used to translate it into needlepoint. Great sweeps of petal are the biggest joy – colour seeping from the darkest recesses to fade like watercolour at the petal's edge. Complicated flower centres can be simplified by a more abstract approach. I've taken liberties with the scale to add drama and set the whole against a twilight blue background with splashes of grey green.

CANVAS	Double thread or interlocked, 7 holes to the inch
DESIGN SIZE	30in x 30in (76cm x 76cm)
STITCH	Random long stitch using 3 or 4 strands
YARN	Paterna tapestry wool (yarn)
NEEDLE	Tapestry size 18
MAKING UP	See Making a Wall Hanging, page 127

SHADE	PATERNA	SKEINS	SHADE	PATERNA	SKEINS	SHADE	PATERNA	SKEINS
Plum	320	11	Fuchsia	354	7	Grape	313	1
Plum	321	5	American beauty	906	2	Violet	304	2
American beauty	900	3	Spice	851	1	Plum	325	5
Dusty pink	911	2	Marigold	800	1	Glacier	562	8
Cranberry	940	4	Autumn yellow	724	1	Glacier	563	11
American beauty	902	3	Butterscotch	703	1	White	260	14
American beauty	904	1	Butterscotch	704	2	Charcoal	221	4
Cranberry	942	3	Cream	263	4	Dolphin	D346	10
Fuchsia	353	2	Basil	D117	2	Dolphin	D389	6
Hot pink	961	8	Grape	312	2	Dolphin	D391	5
Hot pink	962	4	Plum	322	1	Khaki green	644	2

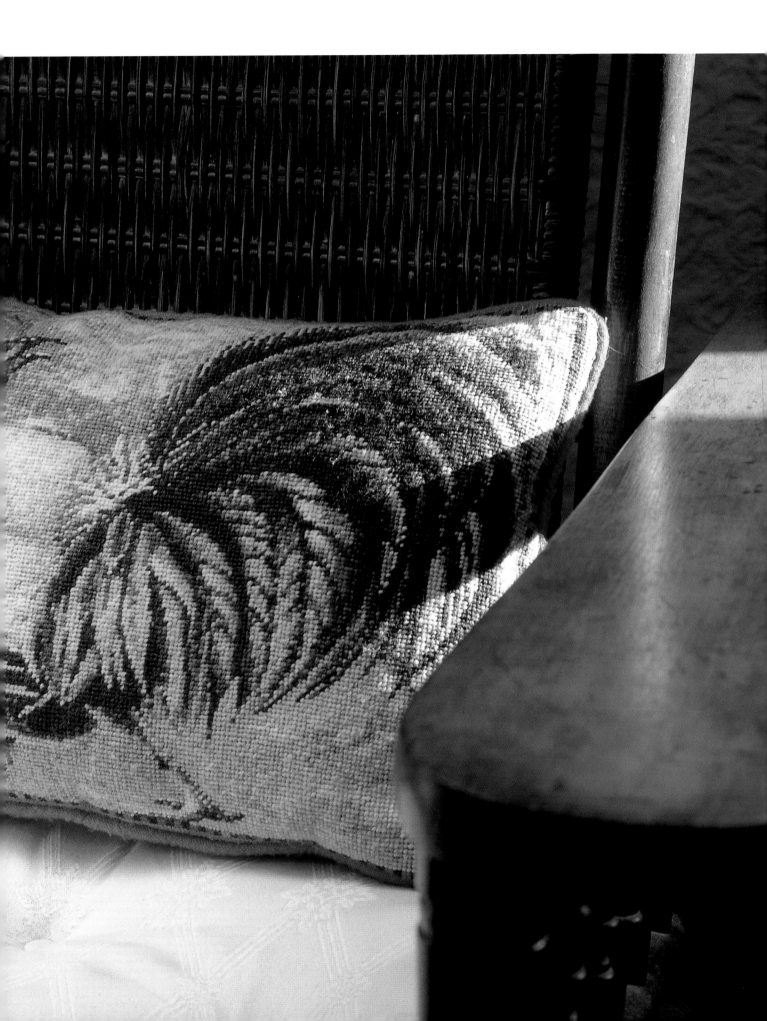

Cockadoodledoo Cushion

'He was like a cock who thought the sun had risen to hear him crow.'
George Eliot (1819–80)

CANVAS	Single thread, 12 holes to the inch
DESIGN SIZE	18in × 12in (46cm × 31cm)
STITCH	Tent stitch or half cross stitch using 1 strand
YARN	Appleton tapestry wool (yarn)
NEEDLE	Tapestry needle size 20
MAKING UP	See Making a Cushion, page 125

SHADE	APPLETON	SKEINS	SHADE	APPLETON	SKEINS
Terracotta	128	1	Sky blue	564	2
Mid blue	157	2	Flamingo	626	1
Chocolate	181	2	Paprika	726	1
Grass green	251A	3	Rose pink	755	1
Orange red	442	1	Bright peacock blue	831	1
Cornflower	463	6	Coral	864	1
Autumn yellow	472	3	Coral	866	1
Autumn yellow	474	2	Pastel shades	876	3
Autumn yellow	475	1	Cream	882	4
Autumn yellow	479	1	Iron grey	964	2
Turquoise	525	1	Bright white	991B	3
Turquoise	527	1	Charcoal	998	6
Sky blue	562	4			

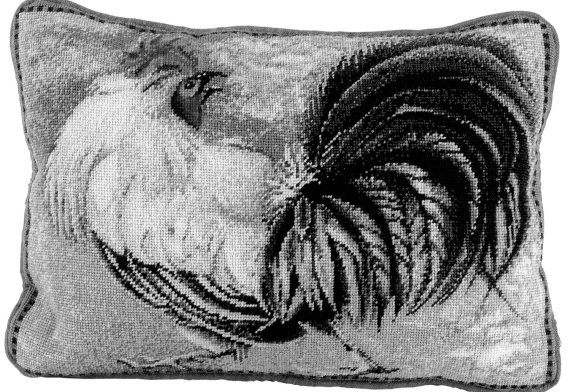

Pansy Mini Cushion

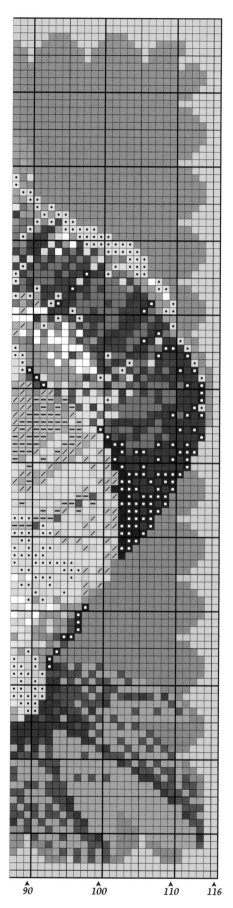

THE PANSY IS A PERFECT choice for a miniature portrait, so neatly filling the format with its smoothly rounded petals, its deep velvety centre. Some of the most beautiful pansies were painted by Henri Fantin-Latour, the renowned French flower painter.

CANVAS	Single thread, 14 holes to the inch
DESIGN SIZE	9in x 9in (23cm x 23cm)
STITCH	Tent stitch or half cross stitch using 1 strand
YARN	Appleton tapestry wool (yarn)
NEEDLE	Tapestry needle size 22
MAKING UP	See Making a Cushion, page 125

SHADE	APPLETON	SKEINS
Dull mauve	935	2
Mauve	607	1
Dull rose pink	148	2
Scarlet	503	1
Bright rose pink	946	1
Autumn yellow	476	1
Bright yellow	554	2
Bright yellow	553	2
Bright yellow	551	2
Lime	997	1
Mauve	601	2
Hyacinth	891	1
Bright rose pink	941	1
Pastel shades	877	2
Bright white	991B	1
Mid blue	156	1
Peacock blue	643	1
Peacock blue	641	2
Hyacinth	893	3

148   476   521   553   626   643   891   991B

156   503   551   554   641   862   929   997

Tulip Mini Cushion

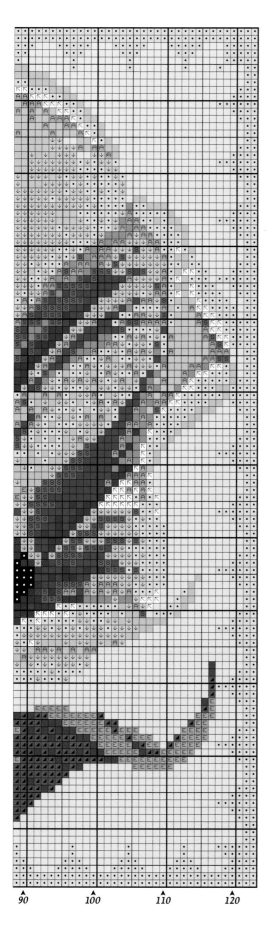

TULIPOMANIA WAS A PHENOMENON that raged in Holland between 1634 and 1637. The culprit was the tulip, newly discovered by European travellers in Turkey. Some flowers were infected by a virus which caused flame-like marks to streak the petals; this delighted connoisseurs and led to outrageous sums changing hands for these specimens. Paintings of the flowers were commissioned and a single bulb could raise as much money as a painting by the grand master of Dutch flower painting, Jan van Huysum.

CANVAS	Single thread, 14 holes to the inch
DESIGN SIZE	9in × 9in (23cm × 23cm)
STITCH	Tent stitch or half cross stitch using 1 strand
YARN	Appleton tapestry wool (yarn)
NEEDLE	Tapestry needle size 22
MAKING UP	See Making a Cushion, page 125

SHADE	APPLETON	SKEINS
Dull rose pink	148	1
Mid blue	156	1
Autumn yellow	476	1
Scarlet	503	1
Turquoise	521	1
Bright yellow	551	3
Bright yellow	553	2
Bright yellow	554	1
Flamingo	626	1
Peacock blue	641	1
Peacock blue	643	1
Coral	862	1
Hyacinth	891	4
Dull china blue	929	1
Bright white	991B	1
Lime	997	1

NAXOS CAT CUSHION

The domestic cat dates back five thousand years to ancient Egypt, where it was worshipped and came to be identified with Bastet, the goddess of fertility – represented in effigy as a woman with a cat's head. So cherished were they that the killing of a cat was punishable by death and when a cat died it was mummified and buried in a special ceremony to the beating of gongs. Seafaring Phoenicians introduced the cat to other lands – to China and India, to Italy and Greece and possibly to Britain.

Cats have inspired love, reverence, fear and hatred. In Europe in the Middle Ages, a long association with death and pagan cults saw millions of cats put to death by the Inquisition and thousands of women suffered the same fate for harbouring them. For the artist however, the cat has held an enduring fascination. They have been portrayed on the walls of pharaohs' tombs and in the pages of medieval manuscripts; been the inspiration of Renaissance art and of gorgeous Japanese prints. Hiroshige, Hokusai and Utamaro, masters of the Japanese woodcut, have depicted their feline agility and playfulness with wit and meticulous observation, inspiring in their turn the French Impressionists and Art Nouveau. Manet modelled many of his cat studies on the work of Hiroshige.

This beautiful cat, seen in Naxos, had immediate appeal. She's very still, head cradled on her front paws. The extended hind leg and curve of tail give an interesting change of direction to the composition. I started with the head and introduced the darks and lights to map out the overall drawing. The directional flow of the stripes created contours describing the rise and fall of the body, the solidity of the leg and the swell of the stomach. The restricted colour range of greys, creams,

bronze and gold with bold black and white touches left me free to concentrate on the intricacy of the markings. It was rather like drawing in pen and wash without the distraction of strong colour – that indulgence I left till last with a rich rust-red ground and a pool of inky shadow to complete the mood.

Naxos Cat Cushion

I CAME ACROSS THIS BEAUTIFUL CAT languishing in a sunlit courtyard in the labyrinthine streets of Naxos. The immediate appeal was the pose she struck and her beautifully defined coat.

CANVAS	Single thread, 10 holes to the inch
DESIGN SIZE	16½in × 13in (42cm × 33cm)
STITCH	Tent stitch or half cross stitch using 1 strand
YARN	Anchor tapestry wool (yarn)
NEEDLE	Tapestry needle size 18
MAKING UP	See Making a Cushion, page 125

SHADE	ANCHOR	SKEINS
White	8006	2
Maize	8038	1
Amber	8104	1
Paprika	8238	12
Paprika	8240	2
Damask rose	8346	1
Raspberry	8424	2
Tapestry green	9054	5
Grey green	9068	1
Brown olive	9302	2
Khaki	9326	2
Cinnamon	9390	2
Oak brown	9404	2
Nutmeg	9448	1
Nutmeg	9450	1
Chocolate	9662	3
Priest grey	9766	3
Granite	9776	2
Black	9800	3

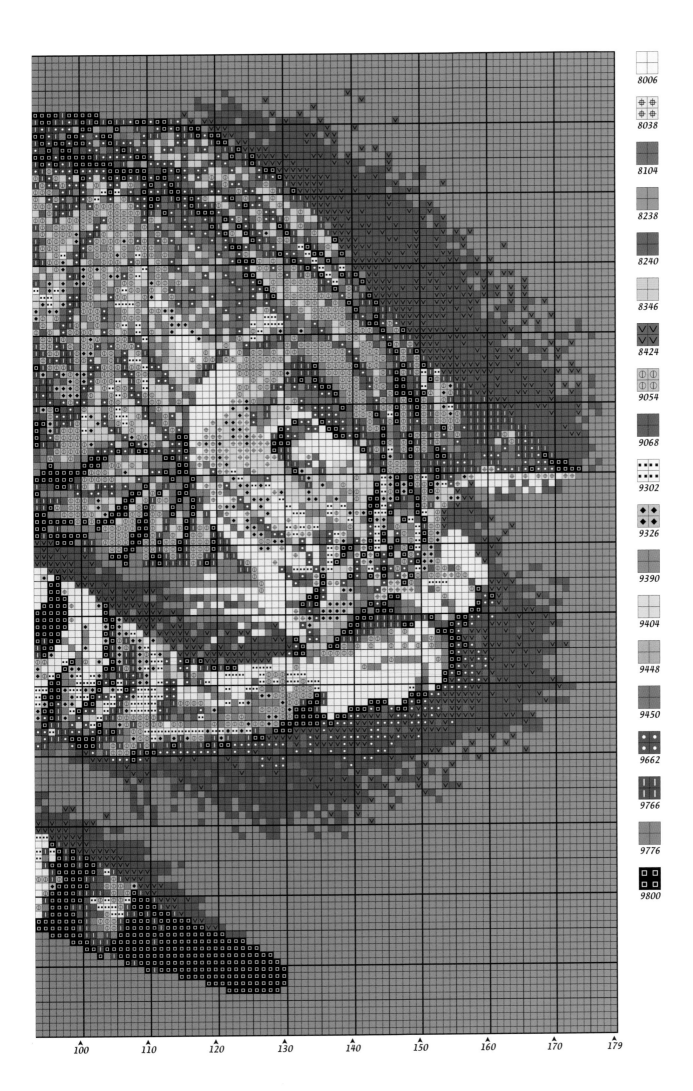

8006
8038
8104
8238
8240
8346
8424
9054
9068
9302
9326
9390
9404
9448
9450
9662
9766
9776
9800

100 110 120 130 140 150 160 170 179

CARMEN MIRANDA CUSHION

The fruit still life is a seductive subject. The Italian artist Caravaggio supposedly produced one of the first examples but the 17th century saw an outpouring of work of this kind across Europe, with Italy, Flanders and Spain as the key centres. Simple, everyday objects were painted with technical virtuosity and a spiritual intensity that makes us slow down and look as we've never looked before.

One of the most important painters of the fruit still life in France during the 17th century was Louise Moillon, who painted almost exclusively the motif of the fruit-laden plate or basket, where different fruits were put together like flower arrangements. She painted deceptively simple compositions with luminous colour.

I have used the pineapple and pomegranate as the two key motifs in my tropical fruit design. Columbus brought the first pineapple to Europe from the West Indies. The native Indian name for it means 'excellent fruit'. The story has it that the Emperor Charles V of Spain was so repelled by its oddity that he refused to taste it. Both pomegranates and figs were known to the Phoenicians, Greeks and Romans. The pomegranate was believed to have mysterious qualities and was used in religious ceremonies, whilst the fig was revered as an important staple food. These ancient fruits figured in both the architecture and needlework of long-dead civilizations.

To these key motifs I've added citrus fruits, grapes, apples and pears to create a visual feast – a cornucopia. A full-scale painting was done first to mark out the general composition and I decided on a semi-circular shape to suggest an abundant pile of fruit. It speaks of exotic origins and foreign climes, of extravagance and the baroque.

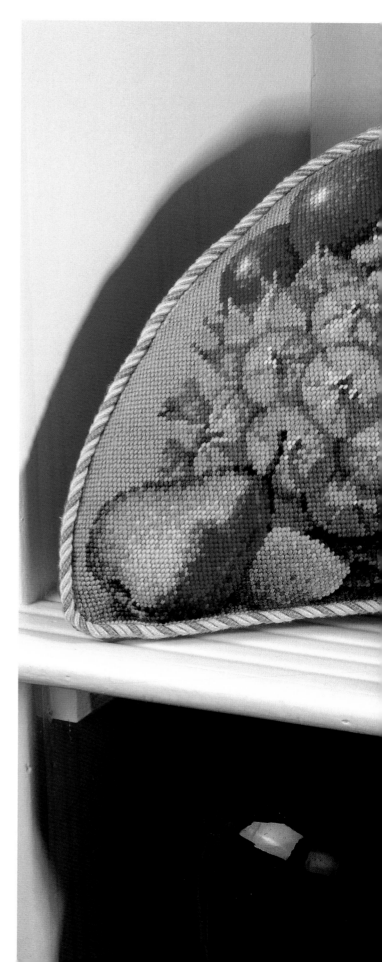

Carmen Miranda Cushion

THEY CALLED HER 'The Lady in the Tutti-frutti Hat', the flamboyant singer-dancer from Latin America. She seduced audiences with her outlandish costumes and gaudy turbans top heavy with pineapples, grapes and bananas. I hope that this exotic cushion will provide as much fun as its namesake, Carmen Miranda.

CANVAS	Single thread, 10 holes to the inch
DESIGN SIZE	23½in × 12¾in (60cm × 32.5cm)
STITCH	Tent stitch or half cross stitch using 1 strand
YARN	Appleton tapestry wool (yarn)
NEEDLE	Tapestry size 18
MAKING UP	See Making a Cushion, page 125

SHADE	APPLETON	SKEINS	SHADE	APPLETON	SKEINS	SHADE	APPLETON	SKEINS
Dull mauve	935	2	Dull rose pink	144	1	Lime	997	1
Wine red	716	1	Pastel shades	884	1	Grass green	251A	1
Mauve	607	1	Honeysuckle yellow	698	1	Hyacinth	895	1
Dull rose pink	148	1	Autumn yellow	476	1	Hyacinth	893	1
Chocolate	186	1	Autumn yellow	477	1	Hyacinth	892	1
Bright mauve	454	2	Autumn yellow	475	1	Mid blue	159	1
Scarlet	503	1	Bright yellow	556	1	Mid blue	156	1
Coral	866	1	Autumn yellow	474	2	Mid blue	155	1
Rust	994	1	Heraldic gold	842	1	Dull marine blue	323	1
Flamingo	625	1	Autumn yellow	472	1	Mid blue	153	1
Flamingo	623	1	Bright yellow	551	3	Turquoise	521	1
Dull rose pink	145	1	Early English green	546	1	Pastel shades	876	1
Mauve	604	1	Early English green	544	1	Bright white	991B	1
Bright mauve	451	1	Grass green	253	1	Turquoise	524	4

Morning Glory Cushion

THIS DESIGN IS A BOUQUET in the Dutch tradition of unlikely bedfellows. I get quite obsessed with my flowers, spending hours making petals curl and reach out. I choose flowers for their languid grace, like tulips and irises; for colours that thrill me, like the intense red of the peony, the deep maroons in the iris, the purples of the hibiscus and the shell pink of the rose. Here, ipomoeas in heavenly blue act as a compositional ploy, gathering it all together – the result is lush and full blown. The background colour could be black, which would be very much in the tradition of Breughel and look equally gorgeous.

CANVAS	Double thread, 10 holes to the inch
DESIGN SIZE	18in x 18in (46cm x 46cm)
STITCH	Tent stitch or half cross stitch using 1 strand
YARN	Appleton tapestry wool (yarn)
NEEDLE	Tapestry size 18
MAKING UP	See Making a Cushion, page 125

SHADE	APPLETON	SKEINS
Mid blue	156	3
Grey green	352	2
Bright mauve	451	1
Bright mauve	453	2
Bright yellow	551	1
Bright yellow	554	1
Mauve	601	1
Peacock blue	642	2
Peacock blue	643	1
Wine red	716	3
Bright china blue	741	2
Fuchsia	801	1
Fuchsia	805	2
Coral	862	1
Coral	864	2
Hyacinth	894	2
Hyacinth	895	2
Dull china blue	929	1
Dull mauve	935	3
Bright rose pink	941	4
Bright rose pink	943	7
Bright rose pink	944	2
Bright rose pink	946	2
Bright rose pink	948	3
Bright white	991B	4
Off white	992	9

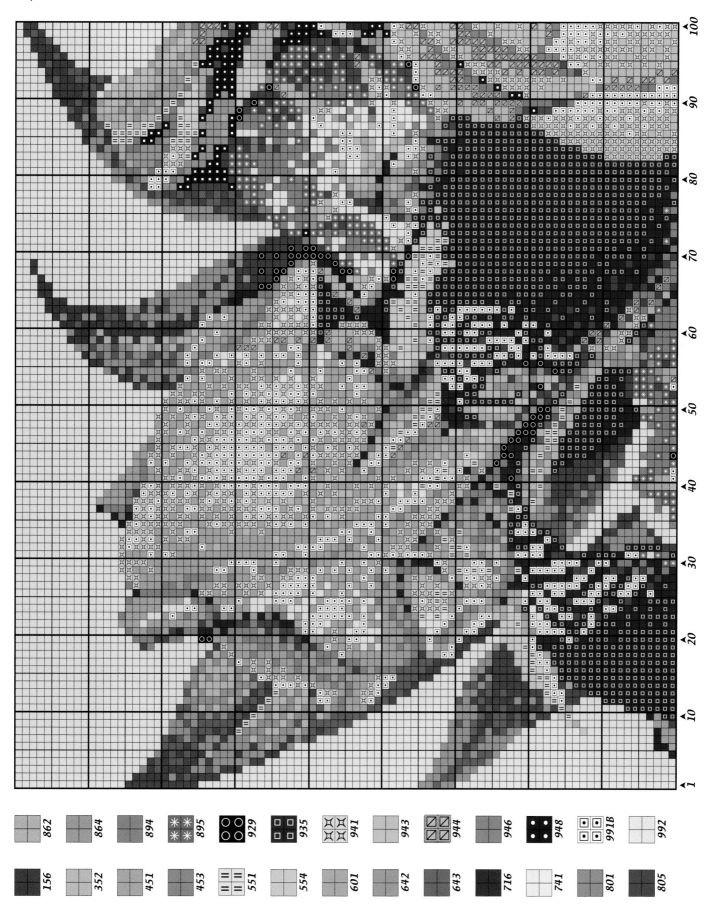

862 864 894 895 929 935 941 943 944 946 948 991B 992

156 352 451 453 551 554 601 642 643 716 741 801 805

Top right

Bottom right

Mandarin Duck Cushion

'The memories of long love
gather like drifting snow,
poignant as the mandarin ducks
who float side by side in sleep.'
Haiku by Lady Murasaki

CANVAS	Single thread, 10 holes to the inch	
DESIGN SIZE	16½in x 13in (42cm x 33cm)	
STITCH	Tent stitch or half cross stitch using 2 strands	
YARN	Paterna tapestry wool (yarn)	
NEEDLE	Tapestry size 18	
MAKING UP	See Making a Cushion, page 125	

SHADE	PATERNA	SKEINS	SHADE	PATERNA	SKEINS
Black	220	4	Mustard	716	1
Plum	320	1	White	260	1
Dusty pink	911	1	Dolphin	D346	1
Rust	870	1	Old blue	510	3
Cranberry	940	1	Old blue	512	1
Copper	860	2	Old blue	513	1
Spice	850	1	Dolphin	D391	1
Autumn yellow	720	1	Glacier	564	5
Autumn yellow	722	1	Blue spruce	533	1
Marigold	800	1	Pine green	662	3
Autumn yellow	727	1	Forest green	602	1
Autumn yellow	724	1	Ocean green	D546	1
Verdigris	D511	1	Pine green	663	2
Honey gold	731	1			
Verdigris	D531	1			
Tobacco	744	1			

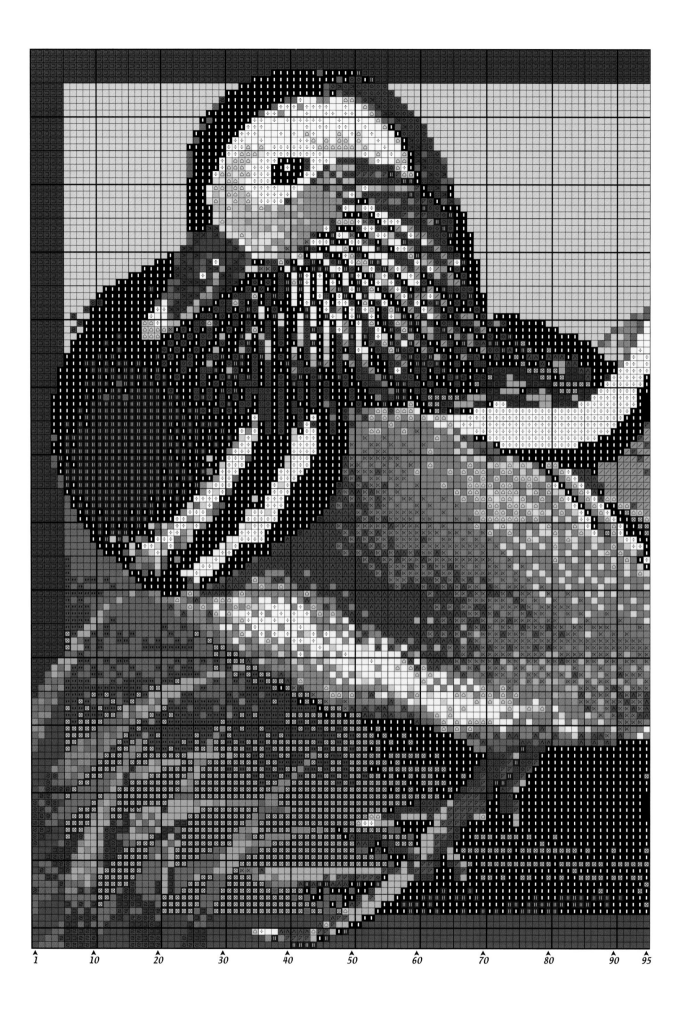

1 10 20 30 40 50 60 70 80 90 95

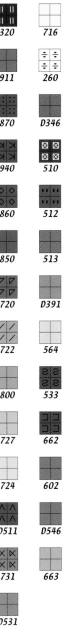

96 100   110   120   130   140   150   160 166

NASTURTIUM WAISTCOAT

Nasturtiums come from the tropical climate of the South American forests and as many as fifty species of wild nasturtiums are to be found from southern Mexico to Chile. The true nasturtium (or Indian cress) is from the watercress family and produces seeds which can be used as a substitute for capers in pickles. It was brought to Europe by the Jesuits who travelled across the world converting 'heathens' and is sometimes called Jesuits' cress. The Latin name, nasturtium, derives from the words *nasus tortus*, meaning a convulsed or twisted nose, due to its pungency. Its peppery taste makes it a popular addition to salads as both leaf and flower are edible. The generic name, *Tropaeolum majus*, comes from the Latin meaning 'trophy' which refers to the likeness of the flower and leaf to a helmet and shield.

The nasturtium is a popular decorative plant in our northern gardens – an old-fashioned favourite, its spurred yellow and scarlet flowers ramble all over the place, a quick-growing screen for unsightly corners. My mother used to cut it almost to the root and plunge it into vases where it would migrate over dressers and flower for weeks.

Names like Tom Thumb and Whirlybird fittingly describe this jester of the flower bed – they're skittish and frolicsome. Tendrils of nasturtiums are often to be found trailing from the base of bouquets and flower arrangements in European still lifes, a space at other times given over to the ipomoea or honeysuckle, which have similar trailing characteristics. Textile designers have embraced them too, for their 'lily-pad' leaf and brilliant colours – so easily lending themselves to stylization.

Nasturtium Waistcoat

MY WAISTCOAT FEATURES a modern nasturtium, a hybrid which includes maroon, cream and dusty pink flowers – a richer, more varied group than the traditional orange. The unmistakable leaf shapes lie like haloes behind the individual flowers in cool blue greens. It's a theatrical flower for a theatrical garment.

CANVAS	Single thread, 12 holes to the inch
DESIGN SIZE	Top of neck to bottom of front points is 24in (61cm)
	Underarm to waist is 9½in (24cm)
	Each front measures 10½in (27cm) across
	When backed it can be altered in size to fit up to
	40in (102cm) bust
STITCH	Tent stitch or half cross stitch using 1 strand
YARN	Appleton tapestry wool (yarn)
NEEDLE	Tapestry size 20
MAKING UP	See Making a Waistcoat, page 126

SHADE	APPLETON	SKEINS
Dull mauve	935	1
Wine red	716	1
Wine red	715	1
Dull rose pink	146	3
Scarlet	504	2
Coral	866	1
Rust	994	2
Dull rose pink	145	1
Dull rose pink	144	1
Bright rose pink	944	1
Flamingo	623	2
Coral	862	2
Autumn yellow	473	2
Bright yellow	554	2
Honeysuckle yellow	693	1
Lemon	996	2
Heraldic gold	841	2
White	991	2
Drab fawn	953	1
Grass green	251A	1
Leaf green	421	1
Winchester blue	853	2
Dull marine blue	323	2
Dull marine blue	321	1
Turquoise	524	2
Turquoise	521	1

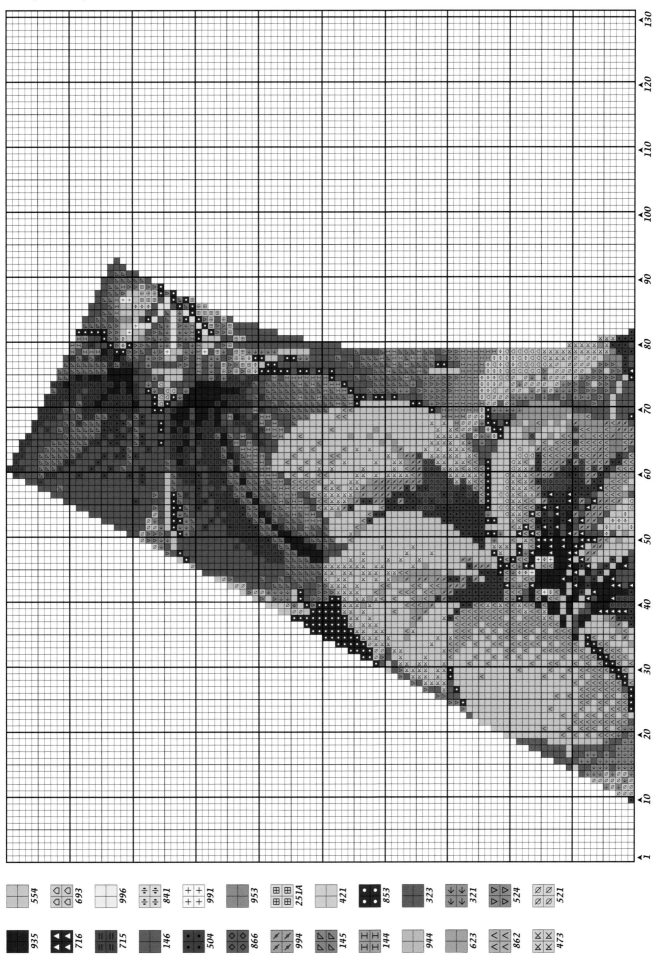

Right panel, top

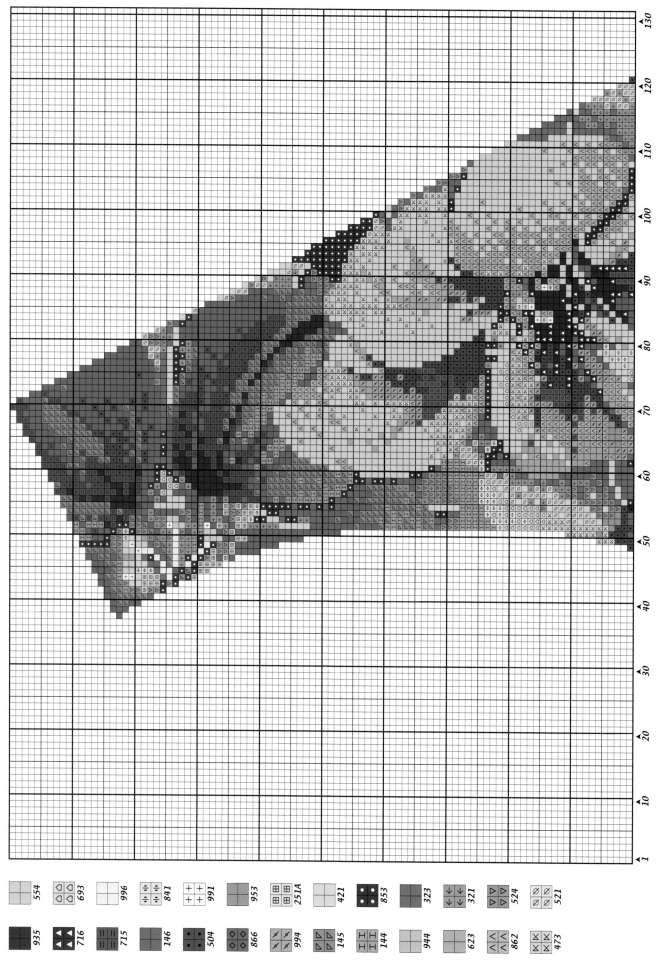

| | 554 | | 693 | | 996 | | 841 | | 991 | | 953 | | 251A | | 421 | | 853 | | 323 | | 321 | | 524 | | 521 |

| | 935 | | 716 | | 715 | | 146 | | 504 | | 866 | | 994 | | 145 | | 144 | | 944 | | 623 | | 862 | | 473 |

Right panel, bottom

FROSTED GRAPES STOOL

Somebody called this design my 'William Morris'. Morris, an English designer and craftsman, worked in the Arts and Crafts movement in the middle of the 19th century. His work was almost exclusively in the field of flat design, seldom venturing into the three-dimensional. Weaving, especially tapestry weaving, was an important element of his work but he found little to inspire him in the work being done at the time. He turned instead to the Middle Ages, in particular to late medieval Flemish tapestries whose flat ornamental qualities particularly appealed to him. With energy and vision he brought about a revival in the craft and his workshops at Merton Abbey survived for sixty years.

Sometimes I tire of hot colours and the softer tones of 'Frosted Grapes' is an example of a more muted palette. Here, I've taken the theme of grapes, nestling like glass marbles among huge vine leaves. Although the original artwork was in paint, I strove for a pastel-like finish, which gave rise to the title 'Frosted'. I could cover a wall with grapes and never tire of them. Dusky pinks, antique blues and limpid greens predominate, with depth conveyed by a pattern-like layering of leaves. Beautiful cream ones float above a layer of blue, the most distant ones denoted with spears of near black – a simple device which creates a quite dramatic sense of space. The background is a cool, unobtrusive pink surrounded on all sides by a braid-like border regimentally spotted in green.

Frosted Grapes Stool

WHILE I DON'T CLAIM any direct influence from William Morris, 'Frosted Grapes' does owe something to the tradition of woven tapestry – a craft I've long been fascinated with and had considerable involvement in. There's a strong emphasis on pattern and the colours evoke the nature of sun-bleached vegetable dyes and cochineal. Its continuous decorative flow well suits a piece of furnishing.

CANVAS	Double thread, 10 holes to the inch
DESIGN SIZE	43in x 14in (109cm x 36cm)
STITCH	Tent stitch or half cross stitch using 2 strands
YARN	Paterna tapestry wool (yarn)
NEEDLE	Tapestry size 18
MAKING UP	See Mounting in a Stool, page 126

SHADE	PATERNA	SKEINS	SHADE	PATERNA	SKEINS
Basil	D127	1	Glacier	562	5
Charcoal	221	6	Forest green	603	2
White	260	2	Shamrock	623	5
Plum	321	2	Loden green	695	2
Plum	322	1	Autumn yellow	724	2
Plum	323	2	Tobacco	744	1
Plum	324	2	Marigold	804	5
Plum	326	5	American beauty	904	2
Dolphin	D346	5	Dusty pink	911	2
Dolphin	D389	5	Dusty pink	912	2
Dolphin	D392	4	Dusty pink	913	2
Golden brown	445	8			
Federal blue	502	17			
Old blue	510	6			
Old blue	511	1			
Federal blue	505	2			
Ocean green	D546	2			
Ocean green	D556	3			

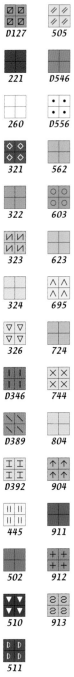

D127	505	
221	D546	
260	D556	
321	562	
322	603	
323	623	
324	695	
326	724	
D346	744	
D389	804	
D392	904	
445	911	
502	912	
510	913	
511		

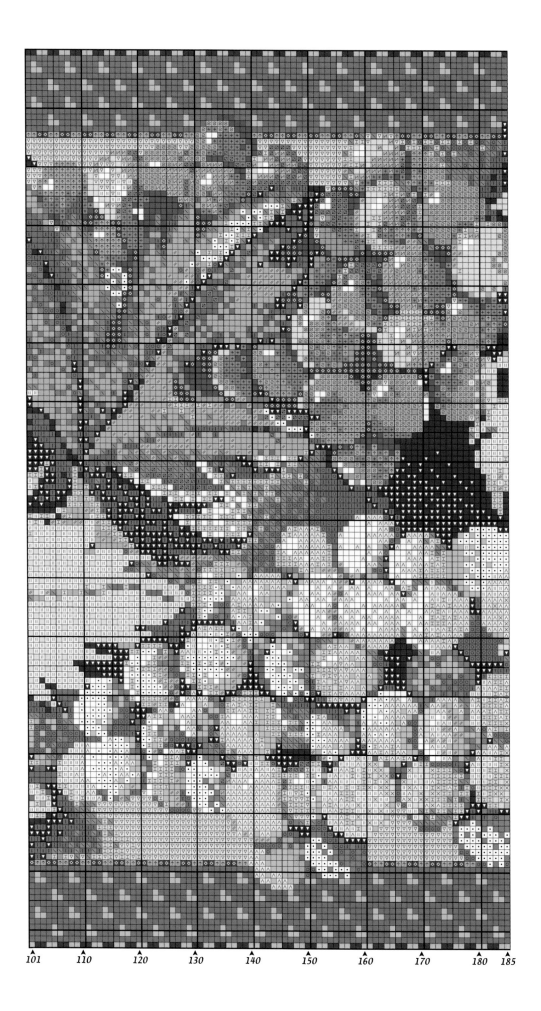

101 110 120 130 140 150 160 170 180 185

186 190 200 210 220 230 240 250 260 270 280 285

D127   505
221   D546
260   D556
321   562
322   603
323   623
324   695
326   724
D346   744
D389   804
D392   904
445   911
502   912
510   913
511

286 290   300   310   320   330   340   350   360   370

371 380 390 400 410 420 430 440 450 456

D127 505
221 D546
260 D556
321 562
322 603
323 623
324 695
326 724
D346 744
D389 804
D392 904
445 911
502 912
510 913
511

ALFRESCO TRIO

The skills of illusion have always fascinated painters. Pliny the Elder praised the painter Zeuxis for such realistic representations of grapes that birds could mistake them for the real thing. Later theologians came to see certain objects as having symbolic and mystical significance and these were used by painters to give coded messages in their work. For instance, flies were considered creatures of the devil; a watch symbolized the vanity of existence; butterflies and dragonflies were associated with the Resurrection and the sunflower with pious people.

This design idea arose from a proposed commission for a Wiltshire church. Grapes have always had a Christian significance and were used in Dutch still lifes to suggest domestic harmony and moral and religious principles. Peaches, which were regarded as a sub-species of apple in the 17th century, had the same symbolism – redemption and victory over sin.

When the church commission failed to materialize I decided to develop the design for my own use. With no symbolic or religious intent, I chose peaches and grapes for this riotous tangle of fruit and leaves. The colours are rich and juicy. It was painted in great detail before I began stitching. I take pleasure in trying to depict something that looks good enough to eat – every grape was carefully rendered, the peaches modelled in mouthwatering tones of orange and gold. It's a sensual experience, an epicurean delight – all my favourite colours set off on a cream ground. The grapes are easier to depict and probably more successful in tent stitch than in the coarser long stitch, but each has its own quality and together the three make an impressive set.

Alfresco Grapes Cushion

'To happy convents, bosomed deep in vines,
Where slumber abbots, purple as their wines.'
Alexander Pope (1688–1744)

CANVAS	Single thread, 10 holes to the inch
DESIGN SIZE	17in x 17in (43cm x 43cm)
STITCH	Tent stitch or half cross stitch using 2 strands
YARN	Paterna tapestry wool (yarn)
NEEDLE	Tapestry size 18
MAKING UP	See Making a Cushion, page 125

SHADE	PATERNA	SKEINS
Basil	D127	1
White	260	1
Cream	263	7
Plum	320	2
Plum	321	2
Plum	323	1
Plum	325	1
Federal blue	506	1
Old blue	513	2
Teal blue	523	1
Blue spruce	530	2
Blue spruce	532	2
Ocean green	D546	2
Forest green	602	1
Shamrock	623	1
Khaki green	642	1
Loden green	694	1
Loden green	695	1
Marigold	800	2
Marigold	804	1
Sunrise	815	1
Salmon	844	1
Spice	852	2
Dusty pink	911	1
Strawberry	950	1
Strawberry	954	1

316 320 330 340 350 360 370 380 390 400 410

D127   623

D234   642

260   694

263   695

320   735

321   800

323   804

324   815

325   844

506   852

513   882

523   885

530   911

532   950

D546   953

602   954

IRIS PANEL

The iris takes its name from the Greek goddess of the rainbow: hardly surprising with its vast range of colours. Showy, extravagant blooms crown sturdy stems furnished with lance-shaped leaves. Long before Westerners took floral art seriously, Chinese artists were painting flowers with dedication and accuracy. Many spent their life painting one particular species.

Japanese artists and designers produced exquisite images of the iris. Hokusai and Hiroshige were models for later European artists who adopted their stylistic devices. Compositions became ornamental, asymmetrical; stems and leaves cut off abruptly by the picture's edge – the tall stature of the iris dictating a vertical format and a stacking arrangement of stems and blooms. Simplified and stylized, the iris filled pages of pattern books for graphic designers at the end of the 19th century. Van Gogh, inspired by Hokusai and Hiroshige, painted the iris with fevered intensity, producing works of drama and emotion. Monet's many paintings of the iris have an airy serenity by comparison.

'Iris Panel' features the bearded iris, the beards bronze and yellow – a sharp accent to complement the purples. Drawn from nature, I painted a full-size study, struggling to keep up with the shifts in the flowers while I worked. Blooms were turned sideways and around, petals propped up with paint-brushes and tape; work done by daylight and electric light with inconstant shadows.

For the needlepoint I used long and short stitch to produce a painterly expressive quality. Bold sweeps are possible, even fine lines and small dots. Colours can be bled one into the other, from the deep velvety aubergines and purples to the antique rose which edges the 'falls'. The effect is rich and satiny, like brush strokes loaded with oil paint.

I've arranged the vertical leaves stylistically as a grid-like backdrop to the fullness of the flowers – the effect softened by the incline of the leaf tips. Spruce blues darken the bottom edge, rising through a band of 'grape'. Regular hatching links the background colours as they move up through a range of blues – dusky at first to duck-egg at the top.

Iris Panel

IN THE FAR EAST, the iris came to be known as the 'victory plant', and belonged to a group of four 'noble plants'. A monk writing from the Yüan period confessed: 'When I am happy I paint the orchid (iris), and when I am angry the bamboo.'

CANVAS	Single thread, 7 holes to the inch
DESIGN SIZE	38in × 28in (96.5cm × 71cm)
STITCH	Random long stitch using 3 or 4 strands
YARN	Paterna tapestry wool (yarn)
NEEDLE	Tapestry size 18
MAKING UP	See Mounting in a Panel, page 125

SHADE	PATERNA	SKEINS	SHADE	PATERNA	SKEINS
Basil	D127	3	Federal blue	506	12
Antique rose	D211	1	Sky blue	585	4
Antique rose	D234	1	Forest green	602	6
Grape	312	1	Shamrock	623	2
Plum	320	5	Loden green	695	2
Plum	321	3	Autumn yellow	724	1
Plum	322	2	Tobacco	744	2
Plum	324	2	Honey gold	733	1
Plum	325	1	Mustard	715	2
Lavender	334	1	Autumn yellow	727	1
Old blue	514	6	Sunrise	815	1
Blue spruce	530	4	American beauty	900	2
Blue spruce	532	7	Wood rose	925	1
Ocean green	D546	4	Toast brown	475	3

Plan of charts

4	1
5	2
6	3

Right

63　70　80　90　100　110　120　130　140　150　160　170　180

| 993 | 716 | 456 | 895 | 805 | 453 | 801 | 948 | 757 | 866 | 626 | 101 | 885 |

| 451 | 884 | 862 | 472 | 861 | 474 | 554 | 996 | 841 | 991B | 156 | 421 | 951 | 476 |

ORCHARD BOUNTY

A parade of colourful names identifies the humble apple – Winesap, Russet, Tremlett's Bitter, Rome Beauty, Granny Smith and Golden Hornet – evoking images of blush red, deep yellow or tart green skin. My Apples bag was originally conceived as a circular shape with a long shoulder strap – in my mind's eye I saw a plate of apples – but a visit from my daughter Anna caused a rethink and we came up with a much more up-to-date, sophisticated shape which I think works beautifully. The apples, maybe Red Delicious, maybe Empire, fill the frame; wine red, touches of rose pink, salmon and gold. I avoided leaves, allowing instead a touch of green around the stems. It's stronger and less fussy and the whole effect, this heap of red apples, is softened and quieted by a subtle dull mauve background which offsets any harshness in the reds. The strap and rectangular base I've kept strictly geometric, a nice counter to the round, full forms of the fruit. This design is a joy to stitch. I had such fun with all the reds. Don't agonize over the close tones of some of the colours. As long as it's tonally correct, your darks and lights in the right places, you won't go far wrong. It would also make a very nice square or rectangular cushion on a coarser canvas to make it bigger. Try a viridian green background – I'm sure I'll be playing around with this design for some time to come.

As with the bag, I've chosen in the Apples and Pears cushion to treat the fruit in a bold sculptural way – with no concessions to the softening effect of leaves or the elaboration of borders. All my efforts went into the modelling of the fruit – the part I find most satisfying.

I could probably admit to a number of influences here – none of them direct but absorbed lovingly over time; the sensual, almost abstract arrangements of red, green

Take a 14in (36cm) bias strip and 14in (36cm) of piping cord. Turn the two long ends under and hand stitch the bias strip tightly around the cord. Then cut this piped strip into five 2in (5cm) lengths.

For the button loops, make five evenly spaced marks along the right-hand side of the centre front, starting below the neck 'v'. Take each of the piped strips, fold in half and position them at these marks, with the raw edges against the centre edge of the waistcoat. Tack (baste) each of these in position.

Measure around the edges and cut a bias strip to this length plus 1¼in (3cm). Cut piping the same length. Fold the bias strip in half around the piping cord. Tack (baste) firmly against the cord edge. With the piping facing away from the seam and raw edges together, pin, tack (baste) and stitch the piped strip all around the edge of the waistcoat. Turn the seams under so that the piped edges show on the right side.

Trim the seams to ⅜in (1cm) and clip corners so that the waistcoat lies flat, clipping seams at regular intervals around all curved edges. Tack (baste) around the waistcoat inside seam line, then press. Turn under ⅝in (1.5cm) around the edge of the lining and then press the lining.

Fit the lining to the inside of the waistcoat. Pin, tack (baste) and hand sew in place. Sew buttons to the left-hand side making sure that they match the position of the button loops. Take out any remaining tacking (basting) stitches.

Making a Wall Hanging

To make a wall hanging you will need: backing fabric (firm cotton or linen canvas); 2oz wadding (batting) (optional); a dowelling rod; and cord or braid.

Cut the edges off the two long sides of the canvas leaving a ¾in (2cm) border. Cut a piece of backing fabric the same size as the canvas. Cut a piece of wadding (batting) slightly smaller than the canvas and tack (baste) it to the wrong side of the canvas. With right sides together, sew the backing fabric to the canvas along the side seams. Turn to the right side. Turn under ¼in (0.5cm) at the top and bottom edge and stitch.

Cut two pieces of dowelling 2in (5cm) longer than the needlepoint width. Turn under top and bottom of the hanging, leaving a gap sufficiently large to house the dowelling. Stitch firmly. Thread the dowelling through the top and bottom. Attach cord or braid to each side of the top rod for hanging.

ACKNOWLEDGMENTS

Generous thanks to all at David and Charles for the team work involved in bringing this book to fruition; in particular Cheryl Brown for the commission and Sandra Pruski for her unfailing good humour which helped enormously; Lin Clements for all her hard work; Ethan Danielson for his magnificent charts; Roger Jury for his friendly co-operation in the making up of the Pansy slippers and Teresa Searle who found time to make up the Apples bag so beautifully. Special thanks to Hugh Ehrman for guidance, support and friendship over ten years and for having belief in me. And to Noel – very special thanks.

SUPPLIERS

Appleton Bros Ltd
Thames Works, Church Street, Chiswick, London, W4 2PE
Tel: 0208 9940711
For Appleton tapestry and crewel wools (yarns)

American Crewel and Canvas Studio
PO Box 453, 164 Canal Street, Canastota, NY 13032, USA
For Appleton tapestry wools (yarns)

Bowhill & Elliott (East Anglia) Ltd
65 London Street, Norwich NR2 1HL, UK
Tel: +44 (0) 1603 620116
Fax: +44 (0) 1603 620066
Email: roger@bowhill&elliott.uk
Website: www.bowhillandelliott.co.uk
For making up the slippers

Coats Crafts UK
PO Box 22, Lingfield House, Lingfield Point, McMullen Road, Darlington, County Durham DL1 1YQ, UK
Tel: 01325 394237
Website: www.coatscrafts.co.uk
For Anchor tapestry wools (yarns), and other needlework supplies

Ehrman Kits
14–16 Lancer Square, Kensington, Church St, London W8 4XX, UK
Tel: 01226 733366
Email: ehrman.kits@btinternet.com
For needlepoint kits, including the following by Elian McCready: Cockadoodledoo cushion; Iris, Pansy and Tulip miniatures; Naxos Cat cushion; Morning Glory cushion; Rose teacosy; Mandarin Duck cushion; Frosted Grapes stool; Alfresco Grapes and Alfresco Leaves cushions; Alfresco wall hanging; Iris panel

Ehrman Tapestry
112 Cross St, Chestertown, MD 21620, USA
Tollfree order line: 888 826 8600
Customer service: 410 810 3032
Fax: 410 810 3034
Email: usehrman@dmv.com
Website: www.ehrmantapestry.com

Paterna Ltd (via The Craft Collection)
Terry Mills, Westfield Rd, Horbury, nr Wakefield, WF4 6HD
Tel: 01924 810812
For Paterna tapestry wools (yarns)

INDEX

A
apple 112–15
Art Nouveau 32
Arts and Crafts movement 70

B
bags 124–5
    Apples Bag 112–14
bamboo 98
beginning to stitch 124
Blake, William 24
blocking 124
Brueghel, Jan, the Elder 44, 46

C
canvas 122
    mounting 123
    preparation 123
Caravaggio, Michelangelo Merisi de 38
Carmen Miranda 40
cat 32–5
cave art 54
Cézanne, Paul 114, 115
chair covers 122
charts, following 123
Chinese art 8, 96, 98
    Ming period 24
cleaning 124
cockerel 16–19
cotton canvas 122
crown imperial 44
cushions
    Alfresco Grapes 7, 78–80
    Alfresco Leaves 7, 78–9, 81
    Apples and Pears 112–13, 115
    Carmen Miranda 7, 38–41
    Cockadoodledoo 16–19
    flower mini cushions 24–31
    making up 125
    Mandarin Duck 54–7
    Morning Glory 44–7
    Naxos Cat 32–5

D
double thread canvas 122
duck 54–7
Dutch painting
    cockerel 16
    flowers 8, 10, 31, 44, 46, 51
    still lifes 78

E
Egypt 6, 27, 32, 54
Eliot, George 18
evenweave 122

F
Fantin-Latour, Henri 29
Fassett, Kaffe 6
Flemish florals 44
fleur-de-lis 27
flower miniatures 24
framed pictures 24–5, 126
frames 123
fruit 7, 38–41, 70–1, 78–91, 112–15

G
Gasquet, Joachim 115
gauge, canvas 122
Genesis 81
Gogh, Vincent van 24, 96
grapes 70–3, 78–91

H
half cross stitch 123
half stitches 122
hibiscus 46
Hiroshige, Ando 32, 96
Hokusai, Katushika 24, 32, 96
hollyhock 6, 8–11
honeysuckle 60
Huysum, Jan van 31, 44

I
Impressionism 32, 96
ipomoea 44–7, 60
iris 24, 26–7, 46, 96–9

J
Japanese art 8, 16, 32, 54, 56, 96
    Edo period 24

L
lacing 125, 126
lighting 123
linen canvas 122
long stitch 6, 10, 78, 123, 124

M
Manet, Édouard 32
Marvell, Andrew 90
mesh, canvas 122
miniatures 24–31
Moillon, Louise 38
Monet, Claude 96
Morris, William 70, 72
mounted panels 96–9, 125–6
Murasaki, Lady 56

N
narcissus 8–11
nasturtium 7, 60–3
Native Americans 54
Naxos 32, 34
needles 122

O
O'Keefe, Georgia 114

P
pansy 24, 28–9, 106–9
peach 78–91
pear 112–13, 115
peony 6, 8–11, 46
piping 126–7
Pliny the Elder 78
Polo, Marco 8
Pope, Alexander 80

R
rose 7, 44–5, 46, 50–1
rug wool 122
rugs 122
Ruysch, Rachel 44

S
seams 124
Shakespeare, William 106
single thread canvas 122
slippers 126
    Pansy 106–9
still life 78, 114
stitches 123–4
stools 126
    Frosted Grapes 70–3
suppliers 127
symbolism 54, 78, 106
synthetic canvas 122

T
tangled thread 124
tapestry wool 122
teacosies 126
    Rose 44–5, 50–1
tension 123
tent stitch 78, 123
threads 122
three-dimensional projects 122
tulip 7, 24, 30–1, 46

U
Utamaro, Kitigawa 32

W
waistcoats 126–7
    Nasturtium 60–3
wall hangings 127
    Alfresco 7, 78–9, 90–1
    Iris Panel 96–9
    Peonies and Hollyhocks 6, 8–11
woven tapestry 6, 70, 72

Z
Zeuxis 78
zip, insertion 125